A RAY OF HOPE
AND
OTHER POEMS

A RAY OF HOPE
AND
OTHER POEMS

K.V.V. Subrahmanyam

STERLING PUBLISHERS PRIVATE LIMITED

STERLING PUBLISHERS PRIVATE LIMITED
L-10, Green Park Extension, New Delhi-110016
G-2, Cunningham Apartments, Cunningham Road, Bangalore-560052

A Ray of Hope and Other Poems
©1989, K.V.V. Subrahmanyam

PRINTED IN INDIA

Published by S.K. Ghai, Managing Director, Sterling Publishers Pvt. Ltd., L-10, Green Park Extension, New Delhi-110016. Laserset at Vikas Compographics, A-1/256 Safdarjung Enclave, New Delhi. 110029. Printed at Gopsons Papers (P) Ltd., Noida, (India)

CONTENTS

FANCY'S FLIGHT

I ambled alone along a winding road,
With life and times a bit bored;
Not because my ambitions heavenward soared,
All prospects blighted and chances marred.
At home I am content with no ills to portend,
To set the Ganga on fire did I never intend,
Nor envy and hate in my bosom ever contend;
Peace and cheer, goodwill and live did I extend,
Yet, what drove me to despair and sorrow ?
Is it because I ponder over the unknown morrow
That an unspeakable pain into my vitals does burrow
Causing thoughts that make my forehead furrow,
Am I a cynic doomed to a mental clinic ?

Does my heart pit-a-pat and make me finick;
My state neurotic worthy of a pathogenic,
Or do I trace this to causes eugenic?
No such ground does appear sound,
We are like springs that are taut and wound
Everyone would like to have his pound;
Envy and hate pile up like a mound.
Live and let live, compassion and cheer
Are traits that are objects of jeer;
We live in an atmosphere of fear,
Human values are things that are dear,
Science has short-circuited the road to doom
The author of small is beautiful was not a prophet of gloom;

Wealth accumulating and men decaying isn't a sign of boom,
For human traits and fellow feeling let there be room.
The age calls for a Messaiah of hope,
Be it a Guru or a master or Pope;
For the spark of the divine let's have ray of hope,
And men with myriad tempers let's know to cope,
This is not lotus-eating day dream,
The pillars of society are its cream;
With notions of nations to mingle and teem,
Onward will it range and flowing into a stream,
Superman is born out of heightened man,
The soul does require spiritual spa and tan,
In the crucible of thought, fancy flightily ran,
Like Alice in the wonderland and Peter Pan.

FLORAL FEUD

'Who is Fairer?' asked the Lotus of the Rose.
'Fair Maids think of me when they want to pose'
Said the Rose and gave unto itself a dose
Of Narcissus-like adulation and became comatose

Having asked the question Lotus didn't deign to reply
But was content with a whitish blush that modestly -
      did Supply;
Which drove the Rose to an umpire to apply
Before whom it wished all its arsenal to deploy.

The fairest of maidens in the Garden of Eve
Those Elf-like charms were meant to startle and deceive,
Was chosen by the contending flowers for a verdict
On their worth, as none could the mind of a woman predict.

It was like Daniel coming to judgment
But then the parties had to marshal their argument;
Rose did strengthen its case and prejudice the judge
Speaking of her cheeks being rosy but the latter didn't budge.

'Who cares for the Rose that is ephemeral?'
Said Lotus with its hue that was chimerical;
Lotus thought white was the symbol of purity
Rose contended that it had better quality.

Lotus is a water-borne flower
That could like the rose glower;
Inconstant rose has its limitation
For it has had many an imitation.

There is yet another rub
No rose but has a thorn;
Lotus has no such nub
As it in watery front is born.

'Lov's like a Red Red Rose'
Said the poet of the scottish land.
Lotus has no such claims bellicose
And the arbiter had a difficult job on hand.

Still she did it in the best of her light
Lotus has the serenity of effortless grace
She decreed 'un-like the rose that parades all her charms bright'
In the victor flower of pride there was never a trace.

Lotus that was meek did inherit the earth
But for rose it was a matter of life and death
Yet the divine umpire ordained rose a place in the sun
Alongside lotus despite the battle that was won.

THE RHIVZHIVIC IMBROGLIO

In a world of torment, with nations in ferment
Is there a ray of hope with wisdom given scope?
Leaders contend with verbiage and accoutrement
Intend on walk on tight rope; world's fate hinged on slope

The pace was hectic, in the region of Arctic
Cheek by jowl with race that is Nordic,
Russians with the bear hug and the dielectic,
And the yankee was aloof with a mien that was mystic

With bated breath people prayed in temple and church
For pacem in terres, for a world sans distress,
Lest atomic warfare leave us in the Lurch
For dame science is a good slave but a bad mistress

The friendly hug and satisfaction smug
Yielded place to polar stares and solar flares,
Ronnie was bitten by the contraire bug
Winsome smile was replaced by hostile glares

The star wars are a symbol of allround might
Leading humankind to a long winter of blight,
With chances of survival ever so slight,
Onward to doom we march in miserable flight.

NUANCES OF NATURE

The query of the century, art or science or both.
But modern man has heart which is loathe
To know of vernal foliage and wooded growth:
To protect nature's bounty ecologist should take an oath

Art is not artifice, science not alien to nature
Flora in forests rear and shelter fauna and many a creature
Living in consort with plants and trees should be a feature
Of life on earth than picturesque scenery that's no better teacher

The dainty clad urban lad
Never saw the sun and the moon and stars;
It's the swain whose heart was glad
At russet sunsets melting into golden bars

In the perennial peregrination of planets
The idylic lover of nature sees sound of sonnets
For him the voice and elan of woodland linnets
Symbolises the psalms of religions and their tenets

Mercury and Saturn, Mars and Venus
Their movements typify celestial battles heinous:
To unravel their mystery is the scientist's onus
The majesty of the bounty of the heavens is a bonus

The feud betwixt nature and art is an eternal tiff
For mundane mortals that are drab and stiff
Ethereal and gossamer shades arc stuff
That may not appeal to traits that are rough

Nature that's delicate and feelings that are tender
Are all gifts and delights that do render
Life worth living and full of joy and wonder
And at the great creator's phantasmagoria ponder

Nocturnal noises of birds and beasts
Diurnal dalliances, loves and hates,
Their lives inundated in primordial feasts
Skyward they spread their wings to heavenly gates

From barren hills and adamantive rocks
Thro' hybrid tendrils, creepers and eglantine stalks
Flower and fruits of varied hues and shapes of barks
Overwhelm the mind's eye with ineffable marks.

FASHIONS SANS SENSE

It's long since we saw a blushing bride
For the Eve of this age has a flushing pride
Of her manners and mores which she doesn't hide
At the altar when the holy wedlock is tied.

Modest womanhood is a thing of the past
In the era of woman lib, it's a cause that is lost
With fashions galore and the world moving fast.
Any surplus coverage of helpless body is like a mast.

'Apparel: oft proclaims the man'
Said the sage of Stratford on Avon;
'Lack of Apparel proclaims the women'
Might well feel those who bemoan.

Maxi, Midi and Mini might lead to nude
When Eve goes all out to display her beauty:
'Handsome is that handsome does'
Is the view of a fogey who makes fuss.

Man's fashion deems him clad from tip to lid
While the fairer sex always makes a bid
Not to provide for her charms a cloak
But to keep on view for all to flock.

The hoop petticoat of the middle age
Did'nt prevent the knights from lusting with a rage
For the fairest of the beauties;
For gallantry was one of their duties.

Woman doesn't charm by dress alone
For the attraction of the sexes is prone
Whether there be parlours for charmers
Or a team of conservative reformers.

In days of yore
We did'nt have fashions galore;
But with raised hips, rounded breasts and scented crest,
With minimum frills they had optimum thrills at their very best.

When will we learn to fortify our culture
Instead of the craze and mortify the vulture
That is deadening our conscience
And making us all persons sans sense?

The scribe may sound a reactionary die hard
Fighting a loosing battle with action rearguard
But shd'nt we try for refinement in taste
And fight a social evil that is a waste?

PRACTITIONERS OF PEDAGOGY

Everyone thinks it's easy to be a teacher
But the profession has many a special feature;
Not all can stand alone and lecture
And manage his wards without any rupture.
All have nothing but respect for the schoolmaster
Have plenty of kindly thoughts to foster,
But who is there to provide him with the tools he needs
And the wherewithal for the mouths he feeds ?
We all agree that the teacher is no mean preacher
But turn taciturn when it's a question of comforts of creature
That make his job worth his while,
And make him do it with a smile.
Why does a teacher have a permanent scowl on his face ?
How shall we make him that frown to efface ?
Do his wards give him the peace of mind
For the many ifs the solution he has to find ?
A society that forever keeps its teachers in tatters
Doth grossly neglect its role in important matters;
For the penury and disdain of one who has taken to the calling
Will a better teacher come out of a better deal
And will the better deal make him get the feel
Of his noble calling and attain professional pride
So that he can make his students fully tested and tried ?
The controversy will last as long as the human race
Whose birth, that of the tree or the seed, earlier took place,
But for us who wish to prosper and ourselves mend
Let's tackle the problem at either end.

Let teachers' day show the body a way
So that the taught will have a better day;
Let teachers' desks be pulpits and their thoughts profound
Let their lessons be sermons and words in wisdom abound.
We want a nation of dedicated teachers
Who will not be pretentious preachers
Whose precepts they themselves will not be breachers
And who indulge in the dichotomy of mean creatures.
What I said may seem pious platitude
That may be attributed to poetic latitude;
But then is not what is required a change of attitude
From the master, and from the students a sense of gratitude?
Are not their genuine teachers who deem their wards as their
        offspring ?
Is not there dedication cause for society's survival and its
        mainspring ?
An inspired teacher is the salt of the earth
An amiable pedagogue spreads knowledge with mirth.
All knowledge towards wisdom should evolve
All that is taught towards this should devolve;
The doubts in the minds of his wards should the teacher resolve
And all pettiness and sloth should the students dissolve,
Then in course of time diligence will bear fruit
And all backwardness and ignorance will become mute
For our country to come out of abysmal darkness
And destroy all weakness in all its starkness
Into that haven of plentitude of effulgence
Should our teachers lead their taught without any indulgence
Thus armed to the teeth with a fund of learning
The bud of our youth will then have a zeal that's burning
They shall then traverse all oceans and voyage all space
Honour all climes that they would grace;
With a fund of confidence life's problems they will face
And all opposition to the ground will they raze,
With such ecstatic hope and pious prayer

11

Let all our teachers grow greyer
Not alone with age but with grey cells
So that divine benediction will ring its bells.

PEACE IS OUR CAUSE

The birth pangs of a nation
Cause considerable exultation
For those who have watched the gestation
And assisted in the operation.
'Sonar Bangla' shouted the sons of the soil
Despite the covetous eyes of those out to foil
A people with a will to toil
And to go through privations for a cause so loyal

Indira was the gynaecologist of India
Whom destiny chose for the people to endear;
She went through fire and brimstone of a monster queer
She met his uncouth billingsgate with a sardonic sneer
Yah Yah Khan 'was the Yes Yes pawn
In the Chessboard that's the international stage;
The Mongoloid smile and the Nixon frown made him fawn
At their feet like a humble page
Chengiz Khan was but a shadow
Of our neighbour with a loot-lust,
Who his hordes from the West did endow
With an insatiable blood-thirst.

How long will the comity of Nations
Continue to dally and show patience
When people of our borders fight an enemy so cruel,
And the people of Bangla Desh go without even gruel ?
How long will the security council

Indulge in words that sound so tinsel
And continue to spectate a spectacle so desperate
With the masses of Bangla Desh in a mood to separate ?
Abraham Lincoln spoke of Government of by and for the
        people;
His country-men would not mind a democracy to topple;
They would fain hug with satisfaction smug
A regime that grave for freedom dug.

In present state of world polity
Will of the people had lost its vitality
For the ills, expediency is a palliation
That is hardly capable of alleviation.

Principles are thrown to the gale
Promises all appear so stale
Personality of world leaders so pale
Wisdom seems to have sunk into an abysmal dale.

When will the world, be fashioned on anvils of peace
When will the scourge of hatred to man decrease ?
Science and technology are at man's feet
Who still thinks of his fellowmen to defeat
Instead of living like brothers recognising each other's work
And leading a life of a contentment and mirth.

When all is said and done
Fighting a war is no fun;
The valiant solider wants many a gun
To do well a job well begun.

The man on the street has a duty to perform
If the jawan at his post has his enemy to disarm;
The wheels of production should revolve by night and day.
The hoarder and the blackmarketeer has to be kept at bay.

14

Every drop of blood shed in the field of battle
Should make us cease to be mere dumb driven cattle
Should kindle emotional impulse to strengthen our mettle
To enable the heroes of our strife their opposition to whittle
For all our martyred sons we should have solemn funeral
That will not be mere biers or corteges but fitting memorial
In the life blood of every Indian to stabilise
The integrity of the nation and every effort to mobilise.

Those who have died have not done in vain
The flower of youth and the prime of age had no personal gains;
They fought for a cause that was dear to their soul
And we require zeal by keeping the country a whole.

Indians of varied faiths should gird up their loins
With a single-minded devotion to save all coins;
To keep the war-machine in a State of trim
For the brave on the borders to ooze with confidence to the brim

The fight is not for a piece of soil or a plot of land
The fight is for a noble cause by a determined band
To thwart an enemy with pinpricks of his brand
At the instance of powers with a strategy so grand.

Despite all these let's pray in mosque and temple
In church and everywhere with a heart that is humble
For our country to come out of the war with ease
For we have always sponsored the cause of universal peace.

STHITHAPRAGNYA

Vain elusive hopes and transient joys
Affect us and we make noise;
Unabashed we display our want of poise
And those around us watch us without choice.

Brittle success swells our head
A little adulation sees us blushing red;
When in a mood, we by our nose are led,
On a diet of sychophancy, we can be fed.

Yet when we find ourselves in a tight corner
We can be likened to a rudderless mariner.
Without mental resources to garner
We think our lot to be that of a mourner.

When we traverse a course that is rough
We lack spartan fortitude that is tough
For our adversaries we are mince-meat of dough,
And many a chance to survive we muff.

The will of the victor one can never vanquish
In twaddle and persiflage he'll never languish;
Igniting the crucible of faith all his anguish,
In steady tread, false steps he knows to distinguish.

Still success and failure, winning and loosing
Cannot be of our choosing;
Failure should not make us a musing,
Sending us into tantrums and abusing.

The sages of diverse faiths do proclaim
That life is a mere exercise to declaim
The soul and exorcise the devil lest it reclaim
The worst in us and its success to acclaim.

The faithful amongst us read scriptures and psalms
To develop in our conscience certain qualms,
Whenever we deviate from decisive norms;
And to detest cant and hypocrisy of all forms.

The world has its share of saints and sinners,
The bulk of the mundane are mere bread winners;
In the race of life they are also-runners,
Without even the chance of winning so much as tenners.

But like the polestar that shines lone and splendrous,
The man with steady wisdom hath a lustre that is wondrous;
Sphinxlike in victory amidst acclaim best thundrous
And solemn in devastation that is horrendous.

SATYA SAI THE MESSIAH

From your ochre robe you radiate light and cheer,
Those that throng to you are filled with fright and fear,
Scared of the ways of the world and Pray, Seer,
Return from you with a heart and mind that are light and clear

Thousands have learnt to bask in your ethereal glow,
Even for sceptics and atheists your love doth flow,
As a gentle stream with silken smoothness and course mellow,
Showering divine benediction on the high and the low.

Thou showeth thy compassion on the unjust and the just,
For thy followers a pilgrimage to thy abode is a must,
For the believers you work wonders with the sacred dust,
For these, faith in thy perennial grace is requisite first.

Disciples alien and Indian are there in plenty for you,
To hear your message which always looks new,
Massive thoughts that are decked in words but a few,
That dissolve our doubts like the sun doth the morning dew.

In this age of desolation, gloom and pseudo reason,
To have faith in higher power is deemed treason;
Yet to thy clarion call our minds do fasten,
And forever does hope and piety on our visage glisten.

HOPE FOR THE COP

Police man's duty is to receive brickbat
For sheer nimbleness he has to be an acrobat,
For blame and praise he should have no regret
Or elation, and in stoic fashion learn all to forget.

When the day's labours are done
And the nights vigil has just begun
We should learn to ponder and prepare
For the morrow's toils without any despair

The arm and the shoulder be strong
While with miscreants in a throng,
His policy should be one of iron hand in velvet glove,
With fervent hope should he learn the lonely furrow to plough

For the policeman critics are not wanting
In his duties he receives many a taunting,
Quite often he feels authorities be more liberal in granting
His tools and perks, the grim finances notwithstanding.

A British cop once had this to say:
'Bobby this and Bobby that and Bobby fall behind,
But please to walk in front, Sir, when there is trouble in the
            wind'
The local minion has nothing more to say.

THOUGHTS ON GANESH PROCESSIONS

Streets choked with bedecked idols
Which would have embarrassed infidels
Watched by wide-eyed kids
With mirth and cheer.
Despite cassandras of atheists
Spreading gloom and jeer,
What is all this trumpet and fanfare?
Doesn't it seem like a warfare?
The pomp and glory of this ostentatious affair
Can hardly conduce to society's welfare.
Mosques are not meant to mask one's bigotry,
Nor temples mere symbols of fanatic idolatry.
Churches not pew-ful of vapourous verbiage
For there will be words abounding sans fruit of sense and
        foliage
In all these shows there's a nuance.
There is no knowing who did collect the finance.
It is sad that for personal pelf to enhance
Many did masquerade doing penance.
Real ethical worth should be ingrained in our blood cells
Not in the mythical, girth of our antideluvian temple bells
For all our religious lore is replete with heavens and hells.
A profound thought, like a smooth pebble, is more than myriad
        shells.

IN DEFENCE OF CRICKET

Despite all the multitudes that throng the cricket field
Some do run down the game with comments veiled,
Talking of ennui and waste of time the spectacle does yield
But on the might of the game their lips are sealed.

Who can deny the game inspires qualities of head and heart,
That call for discipline of mind and body of a high sort,
That spin bowling is a fine art,
That close in catches needs one to be agile and smart?

The sound and fury of pace and swing
Doth the death knell of many a batsman ring;
To face real pace one has to bring
Guts and gumption which is no mean thing.

The game reflects the philosophy of life
The ups and downs are mirrored in the strife
In the middle, where rivalry is rife
And everyone awaits a chance to snipe.

A renowned batter may make a duck
And throw all his ills on dame luck;
All because he didn't avoid the snick
And went for a venturesome flick.

History is made and records are broken
And all these denote a token
Of blood and sweat and limbs that are shaken
And dauntless deeds bespoke of efforts that didn't slacken.

Travails and trials are the tales of tastes,
Success or failure on a flimsy thread rests;
None dare hope to feather their nests
For all time to come and figure in the lists.

Exploits on the field have been sung by many a literary name
Battle of ball and bat has brought the wielders fame;
Cardus and Gardiner have penned the glory of the game;
For the true connoisseur success or failure is all the same.

For witnessing the Test in cricket
There will be many a pest for ticket;
For the thrill of the fall of a wicket
The addict would fain empty his pocket.

Whatever the critics may ascribe
And deride the game in terms to describe
The true devotee would continue to subscribe
To the game, with worthy mementoes to inscribe.

THE GENIAL COPPER

For all his friends he was Joe,
Wherever he worked he never had a foe;
To those with requests he never said no,
Stranger he was to cunning, mean and low.

To one and all he kept an open table,
Even to his detractors he was always noble;
All his cunning he confined to the bridge table,
He encouraged all those who were keen and able.

Ever a connoisseur of sports and games,
Those from humble beginnings but now with big names
Have gotten his kindness and help in trying times,
Worthy to be extolled in these humble rhymes.

For a calling he chose to be a copper,
In any other line he would still have been a topper;
But in times as these may have been a cropper,
Where discretion was needed he was ever a brick dropper.

His manner endeared him to his men,
He'd a shrewd mind to gauge all things in his ken;
Precise and matter of fact were the notings from his pen,
Men of myriad tastes gathered in his den.

There was Hasan, the wizard of chess,
The Golf coach from Delhi lodged in the police mess;
With all his versatility there was never any fuss
In his mien, though he was always in a buzz.

Gentle and kind to all he met,
He was ever amiable without hindrance or let;
Wander-lust was in his eyes ever set,
Around him was a genial aura and air of well met.

Queer was the assertment of men he had around,
In mirth and merriment they did abound;
Elan and espieglerie they spread all round,
The glory of cheer together they found.

Bridge and Golf amongst the games did he live,
With the princes of these games did he often move;
To catch up with tourneys he was always on tow,
But in postmortems never was there rancour or row.

Here was a thirsty and restless soul,
Who was alien to language that was foul;
With him prince and pauper sat cheek by jowl
In an age being good which is neither fish nor fowl.

ON THE JUBILEE

A quarter of a century hath passed
Since the shackles of serfdom were lost;
'tis but a tiny speck in the ocean of time
But just cause for me to break into rhyme.

The pantheon of patriots that put us on the path
To peace and progress knew no sloth;
They labour'd with devotion round the clock
Despite Britisher's efforts to block.

Jalianwallahbagh and the Rowlatt Act
Are dark pages of history in fact
Bhagat Singh and his tribe of sartyrs
Made the tyrannical rulers appear as satyrs.

The biblical span of three score and ten
Has this century in its ken.
Who in the early decades could
Say when Indians would get out of the oppressors' den?

The twenties saw a gleam of light
Though feeble and hardly bright,
The slender form of the Mahatma induced a light
That in days to come British fortunes did blight.

It was not a one man show
As the country had a veritable row
Of spirited men with a vow
To free their motherland they did love.

There was the spectacle of the round table
Which showed the Britishers merely tellling a fable;
With the fate of Indians did they continue to gamble
By a reign of terror that was typical of John Bull.

'Blood and Tears, toil and sweat'
Were the slogans of the leader of Allie's War,
Lo and Behold, They continued their stranglehold
And to tarnish democratic image they went far.

The movement reached its height in the Forties
When the Nation sent its Satyagrahis in sorties
Despite the Ruler's effort to administer a fright
And cow down the determined bond with his might.

Cries of 'Quit India' rent the air in the ides of August
The world watching the region of terror was aghast;
Prophets of doom could portend nothing but gloom
Shadows of prison houses were only things that did loom.

The cream of the country could dream only entry
As proud members of the comity of Nations:
The sons of the soil and the gentry
Were at the tether-end of their patience.

Fifteenth of August is a Red Letter Day
That should be remembered by young and old,
For the heroic deeds of the humble paved the way
In a manner which should be writ in letters of Gold.

Our Memory of their deeds is getting rusty
Our National fervour is getting musty
We seem to be busy with our petty Squabbles
Devoting the bulk of our time in rousing rabbles.

We are still a long way from the promised land
The ever-green Eldorado of our struggling band
Of leaders eager to give every man
And every section of people a fair deal.

For all this, let us have our feet firmly on the soil
And realise that there is no ephimerical Alchemy
Except an indelible faith in the magic of toll
With a determined bow to treat all sloth as blasphemy.

HOMAGE TO MOTHER, JILLELAMUDI

Dear art thou to thy devotees, Mother
Whom with affection you did always smother,
Everyone before you felt like sister and brother,
You taught your folk to love one another.

Kindness you had for all in boundless measure,
A few moments with you your followers did treasure:
Rid did they feel of world's problems and pressure,
Released their foreheads of furrows and fissure.

From your presence emanated an ethereal glow,
Compassion and solace in abiding level did flow,
In a world of tumultous gusts that blow,
The tensed nerves and pace of life render slow.

Some may feel what you left is a void,
Their pent up emotions get taut and buoyed;
With the queer quirk of fate they get annoyed,
For they can't conceive a world with you devoid.

Yet, thy silent countenance and soothing words shed a light
That not all the illwinds that blow can blight,
For thy divine residue of power has a might
That nothing on earth can slight.

Let those who worshipped Thee in human form,
Have infinite faith in Your curative power that's balm,
Grant them inner peace and tranquil calm,
To counter world's onslaughts and many a storm.

NATION OR NOTION

The Sikhs have always been a martial race
By gallant acts they set ablaze
A trail of glory, deeds of daring and grace
In fields of battle and border frays.

Warm in heart and candid in talk
Old and young they've a soldierly walk,
With sprightly presence in every bivouac
And victory their efforts did never baulk.

What became of all these saga and action?
Why did they fall a prey to scheme and faction
Are all their glories mere legend and fiction
Heer and Ranjha, all empty drama and diction?

Aliens scoff at India not a nation but a notion
Are the wounds of fraticidal flights washed by lotion
Of Speeches, resolves and police in perpetual motion;
All these and yet the country's cause has no promotion.

Gandhi and Nehru, Patel and Tilak all fought
For something better than empty squabbles me thought
All their torrid eloquence ended in a drought
Of aridity and endless troubles we bought.

They say darkest cloud has a silver lining
The historicists ever for good old days pining.
Despite the fact the good and the bad intertwining,
To ferret out gold and silver we sh'd go amining.

We are not alone replete with ills
All countries have problems with rumour mills
Modern man has tensions upto the gills
Despite all the window dressing and frills.

Still amidst us are Amtes with zeal
Who for the people's cause have a feel
To cater to the starving with a meal
And run the ship of state on even keel.

Let the young come out with work and zest
And uphold values that are best
Instead of staying crouched in a nest
And for all society remain a pest.

This is the time for all men to have a vision
And work for uplift with a national mission
Create a climate to work with a passion
To realise the dream of India, a well knit nation.

TRACING TEACHERS TRAVAILS

Examination is an abomination and a damnation
Ordained the arbiters of the destiny of the Nation.

The bureaucrat and the merchant
The plutocrat and the pauper
Deplored with penchant
The dangers of the questions paper

How will the teacher maintain
Discipline sans power to detain?
How will the student obtain
Recognition of the worth of his brain?

Will classroom be all venues
For wars of attrition?
Of will then be stuffed with parvenus
In many a position?

When a teacher of chemistry explains ammonium hydroxide
How is he to contain his wards from pandemonium alongside
Without even so much as a pretension
Of a possible detention?

If the eves in the classroom, ever eye the chronometer
Sitting perfumed cheek by painted jowl—ready for a cosmetic
    daub.
And boys react like a charged battery—kicking the needle of
    the ameter.
Ever on the alert to constitute—with the girls a composite mob.

How then will the teacher manage
The girls and boys without damage
To his name and reputation?
If the pedagogues to the needs of the pupils must minister
In the light of an ukase so sinister
Can they but go on a deputation?

A harassed master thought faster
Than his clan and suggested
The chief minister for a brief semester
Tend his flock and disgusted
Perhaps the latter would fain exchange places
And for all I know the state would go to blazes

Teach not lest thou become taut
Test not lest it be thy fault,
Query not lest you become weary,
And read not lest you become dreary.

Thus the Bible may point our foibles
The ten commandments may improve our deportment
But this our education reform will cause subjugation uniform
In the devalued degrees of our ineffectual department.

NEW YEAR MUSINGS

Nineteen hundred and Seventy Eight —
Will it be a year that's happy and bright
Or one of problems that give us a fright,
And pose a spectacle of depression and blight?

Soothsayers and stargazers foretell things to come,
Instil a paroxysm of eerie feeling making us numb,
With their spiritual aura render us dumb,
But for progress and plenitude there is no rule of thumb.

'Qui judicatis terram diligite justinium',
Rest is shibboleth causing pandemonium;
In common parlance it's justice tempered with love,
When the world will be a better place than now —

Men are many prescribing short cuts to success,
Crackpots who commend jackpots are in excess,
Lovers of currency are many among the light-fingered gentry,
The conscience-stricken thro' lotteries try to put in an entry.

For the Timorous, the new year will be full of fears,
The slightest sigh or sob will move them to tears;
But for those endowed with guts and courage
All sorrows and worries seem but a mirage.

Critics of our actions will not be wanting,
Ever with their barbs will they be taunting;
The prophets of gloom will ever be chanting
The forebodings of doom with raving and ranting.

They should'nt deter us from doing what we deem right,
With a heart and soul, saying to ourselves, come what might,
So long there's flesh and blood, skin and bones,
All sh'd ensure amongst us there are no drones.

What we do, may at times err,
But so long there is effort, it is no slur;
In our scheme of things, sloth and self-pity have no place,
For those who strive there will ever be divine grace.

The year that is past had seen changes vast,
Not to speak of calamity that left us aghast,
Still, we deem it a curate's egg that is good in parts
And take it as philosophy that life imparts.

New Years are full of resolutions,
Alas, the morrow thereof melts into dissolutions;
Yet it is better to fight and fail,
Than give up the ghost as of no avail.

A RAY OF HOPE

Years two and decades two are gone
Since the Republic of India was born
For the aspirations of the people 'twans dawn,
After the night of serfdom it was morn.

Nineteen thirty was the year of the Round Table
Which show'd the Britishers to be tellers of many a fable,
All the freedom fighters with their lives did gamble
To give the alien rulers of their patriotism a sample.

Thirties and early forties were years of suffering
When young and old men and women were ever offering
Their all and their lives for a cause so dear
And collecting in thousands their leaders to cheer.

With the dawn of freedom and partition came the massacres
Leaving a trail of bloodshed and bitterness that left wiseacres
Wonder whether our integrity will last
Or our glory will only be a thing of the past.

But the Father of the Nation his soothing balm did employ
And on the dark spots of savagery his followers did deploy
All their wonted compassion in a spirit of dedication
Lo and behold! Ere long there was a shower of divine
       benediction.

Not long afterward The Mahatma was felled by a shot
That on whole humanity was an indelible blot;
The departure of this great soul stunned the country as a whole
Into sense enough to remind them of their goal.

Fifties and sixties were decades of uneasy peace
In our relations with China and Pakistan we were ill at ease
Though on the domestic front we bore the brunt
Of the costly wars with an ease that was not our wont.

We built many a dam and a project
As strengthening our economy was our object;
During centuries of alien rule we were a nation subject
To a tyrannous regime that left us in penury abject.

Socialism we have sworn to be the pattern of our existence
In simple parlance it would mean a level of subsistence
That would make us hold our head high
In a manner that was till now impossible wellnigh.

Let this our national day remind us of the long way
We have yet to traverse before we can proudly say
That we are a people contented and gay
Which for the benighted nations would constitute a ray.

NEHRU, THE DREAMER OF DREAMS

1. Hypocrisy, hails the Adage,
    Is nothing but the homage
    That vice pays to virtue;
    It's a quality that we should eschew.

2. But, then, who is not a hypocrite,
    The man who adulterates his concrete,
    Who his ill-gotten wealth doth secrete,
    Who the states' coffers doth deplete?

3. What of the pious who avoid taxes
    The man of religion who eloquent waxes
    Who has jingling of coins in vaults and boxes
    Ar'nt his ilk the bane of society? Foxes.

4. What of the departments full of babus
    For whom work is one of the taboos
    When administration is lax and loose
    When anything can be got done by means of booze?

5. But to speak of the father of the nation
    Is for one and all a fashion;
    Despite the new rich with increase in station
    We grovel in dust causing curious exultation.

6. Jawahar walked in the footprints of his master
   He talked cautioning us against the disaster
   Of slipping into a morass of narrow-mindedness
      faster
   Than we knew, and of ideals and goals to foster.

7. An internationalist to the core that he was
   Nothing mean or plebian did his lips ever pass
   With a sangfroid, he was never at a loss
   And in dealing with masses he was always the boss.

8. Communal frenzy and caste clique
   He wanted to root out from the public;
   He ever sensed this danger however oblique
   For he thought integrity of the country unique.

9. As a purveyor of world history
   For him peep into future was no mystery;
   'A dreamer of dreams born out of due times'.
   He was a visionary worthy of the best of rhymes.

10. To commemorate him we celebrate children's day
    So that we can put into the embryo of today
    His noble thoughts and deeds to show the world a
       way
    To live together, to keep envy and hatc at bay.

PANCH SHEEL OR PANCH TANTRA

There was a cat called Mao
That sat on a great wall
And all the world couldn't know
Which side it would fall.
Mao and Chou had a pow-wow
With a hyena called Henry and   vixen called Nixon;
The cat and the canary made them kowtow
Despite the latter's protestations in plausible diction.
The fulminations of the foursome
Caused a situation that was loathsome;
Though cloaked in a communique that seemed winsome
They didn't create an atmosphere that was wholesome.
The bear and the bull dog
Could ill afford to go the whole hog
With the American fox and his security cop;
They knew the trip to catland was a flop.
Taiwan to the winds did they throw
Pak and India they did'nt want in friendship to grow;
On Vietnam and Korea they agreed to disagree
But in Bhutto they found an animal with pedigree.
Nixon and his conscience keeper heaved with satisfaction to the
        brim
Little knowing the position they made grim,
Pattern themselves on their being able to trim
And fathom the depths of a phenomenon so glum.

They thought they sublimated the yellow peril,
They found a clue to the Chinese puzzle
They dismissed all talk of Red China as devil,
They were trapped in the trip in a euphoric nuzzle.
The Chinese potentate summed up his indoctrination in the
    words of Panch Sheel,
The cloaked dagger with an oriental design he could well
    conceal
From his guests, who couldn't see the difference
Between Panch Sheel and Panch Tantra; to show their
    preference.

SAGA OF THE SPINNERS

There was no chance for Wadekar,
Said the Captain of the English side;
But the First Test was a breath-taker
Brimful of suspense and swing of the tide.
Illingworth won the Toss
Wadekar thought was a loss;
Luckhurst and the rest of them all
Before the mighty spinners had a fall
Yet the battling of John Snow
And the Spartan will of the English captain
Meant many a furrow of the brow
Of the Indian batsmen.
'Twas the lofted late cut
That was mopped up by Venkat
At slip ever so agile
Making batsmen look fragile,
The weather God shortened an inning
Of Solkar in mood of winning;
With not out Bats Chandra and the Sardar
Illy's hope of win could go no farther;
The second day England at its best
The skipper himself with Luckhurst
Went about the Indians with a thirst
And the runrate almost a cloud burst.
The cloud burst indeed dealt a cruel blow
With English seamers bowling with a glow
And a sprakle and a pace

To Indians that was a menace
The last of the test matches
Was famous for its catches.
Hutton for runs appear'd a glutton
Only till Chandra was put on
And their meagre stock laid bare
It was Chandra's match chroniclers w'd say
As he made batsman after another essay as
A stroke that was not there
Chandra had a top spinner
That was a match winner
That tied Knott into many a knot

That made Fletcher his copy book blot
He bowled an exceeding good googly
Albeit with an action so ugly
But the eating of the pudding being the proof
One saw batsmen going back with a look of reproof
Still the English wielders of the willow
Did indulge in stroke play so mellow
That made many a connoisseur bellow
The batsman was a jolly good fellow
Knott did have a happy trot
With a plethora of strokes he brought
Runs to England for a total to amass
Sufficient to humble indians en masse
Never did the India beat the Windies
Never did Calypso succumb to the rope trick
As when Wadekar and his men
Did Herd the lion in its den.
John Bull with a determination so full
Did try the Indian edge to dull;
By hook or crook
Alas' the disaster was too bad to brook.
Hail thee thou Champion of champion sport

Let's quaff with champagne and loud report
With goodwill and admiration to support
The victor of the game in every port,
All this thanks to selector called Merchant
Despite all detractors so trenchant
Picked the right men with a penchant
And named a team that was to enchant.
With this, will we have more of cricket in politics
And less of politics in cricket
With a single minded zeal at the wicket
With success in all fields to beget.

SAGE OF KANCHI

Thou self effulgent light forever shining bright
Givest succour of abode for those in a plight
With supreme spiritual prowess that is thy might
That suffuses thy followers at thy mere sight

We bask and glow in thy beneficent flow
Of love and benediction to the high and the low,
On our march to bliss thro' steps sure but slow
On thy well chosen path for ever to follow.

Thy precepts are noble, thy example a fable
Of austere life and august thoughts a table
Of pious deeds and soothing words that enable
One and all to rise above the levels of the rabble

From North to South, from Cape to Mount
Thou hast wandered on foot and been a fount
Of ethical nectar to followers without count,
With thy moral tone as is thy wont.

From tip to top from head to foot
Bathed in ethereal dharma upto the root
Thy presence exorcises all the dirt and soot
Of the soul and cleanses the stuft bosom to boot.

Thy mentor the original sage of Kanchi
Sent one and all who saw Him into spiritual frenzy
Since thy physical age was hardly twenty
With religious fervour and guts plenty

Armed thus with human in divine form
You practised and preached tenets of pristine norm,
On your flock you showered love and blessings uniform
With an eye on redemption and spiritual reform.

Heaven descends when earth overflows with filth
Vulgar forms of avarice and bestial stealth
And cunning whelm men whose quest for wealth
Forebodes nothing but bottomless perdition and illth.

Thus spake the song celestial *Gita* the holy
Whoever ignores it does only out of folly
And on the doomsday our balance of piety should tally
Lest our record book with *dark deeds* sully.

Again we turn to thy wisdom mellow
To guide us not in sin and crime to wallow
Not to chase shadows and successes that are hollow
But to seek steady wisdom and transcendent halo

Though young in age for a sage
Thy penance reflects solemn visage
Authenticity marks thy message
How for thy purpose is ailments to assuage

May the Lord of the universe sustain thy rule
For generations, the saviour of soul,
And path maker to spiritual goal,
Counsellor alike in delight and dole.

SHAKTI - THE DIVINE MOTHER

In the song of the bird, in the etymology of the word,
In the eye of a storm, in the expanse of a farm,
In the freshness of a stream, in the sweetness of a dream,
In the smile of a child, in the forest of the wild.
In the depths of sorrow, in the hopes of the morrow,
In the length of a shadow, in the glade of a meadow.
In the fulness of a flower, in the steepness of a tower,
What do we see but your glory and your power?
From the burden of ages of the wisdom of sages,
From the Himalayan heights to herculean fights,
From wayward wastrels to wandering minstrels,
From dangling crooks to gambling flukes,
It is thy writ that runs large and eternal
For thy devotees you abound in affection maternal.

A POET'S PRAYER

In this Conclave of the purveyors of verse
There should be none for flights of fancy averse
To Portray Picturesque Poems of Perennial Rivers
Or a object d'nture meadows and valleys diverse

The poet the lover and the lunatic are of compact
Spake the Bard of Avon; yet for literary impact
The song of the muse and the psalm of the poet
Are things that spread serenity and quiet

Let the writers of the world over unite
The hearts and minds of people with love and cheer ignite
Unearth friendliness and bonhomie like mining of lignite
And dispel the enveloping gloom of darkness and night

Humankind should be replete with sweetness and light
Though politicians indulge in quibbling with all their might
For self aggrandisement they trade in eternal fight
The lips of men of goodwill seem sealed tight

The power of the atom leads us to doom
Fate of men and destiny of earth do largely loom
Not only for economy there is depression and boom;
For complacency and lotus eating let there be no room

Kipling and Kafka, Wells and Orwell
Did to historicists bid forever farewell,
In futuristic visions of science fulfilled revel
In the blissful dreams of days to come marvel

Poetry is airy something substantial nothing say
The deriders of the muse, if they had their way
For those not in the art and merely persons lay
Cannot divine the depths of the muse and feel gay

Yet for the prosaic all is not lost
For time to come, future present, and past
For those in their prime of life that is fast or well past
In moments of crisis Parnassus provides a mast

Whether to extol a love or deride a hate
To praise one's fortune or pity one's fate
One can pierce thro' heaven or peep into hell's gate
To dip into poetic manna it's never too late

In this the hospitable soil of Thais, to the muse
Let's all sing hosannas and vibrant cultures fuse
In many splendoured foliage with brightness of leaves in dews
Offer universal prayer in Wats with views and churches with
        pews